MULTICULTURAL SEASONAL CRAFTS

AUTUMN CRAFTS FROM DIFFERENT CULTURES

12 Projects to Celebrate the Season

BY MEGAN BORGERT-SPANIOL

a Capstone company — publishers for children

Raintree is an imprint of Capstone Global Library Limited, a company incorporated in England and Wales having its registered office at 264 Banbury Road, Oxford, OX2 7DY – Registered company number: 6695582

www.raintree.co.uk
myorders@raintree.co.uk

Hardback edition © Capstone Global Library Limited 2023
Paperback edition © Capstone Global Library Limited 2024

The moral rights of the proprietor have been asserted. All rights reserved. No part of this publication may be reproduced in any form or by any means (including photocopying or storing it in any medium by electronic means and whether or not transiently or incidentally to some other use of this publication) without the written permission of the copyright owner, except in accordance with the provisions of the Copyright, Designs and Patents Act 1988 or under the terms of a licence issued by the Copyright Licensing Agency, 5th Floor, Shackleton House, 4 Battle Bridge Lane, London, SE1 2HX (www.cla.co.uk). Applications for the copyright owner's written permission should be addressed to the publisher.

British Library Cataloguing in Publication Data
A full catalogue record for this book is available from the British Library.

ISBN 978 1 3982 4542 6 (hardback)
ISBN 978 1 3982 4541 9 (paperback)

Editorial Credits
Editor: Jessica Rusick
Designer: Sarah DeYoung
Originated by Capstone Global Library Ltd

Image Credits
Project and materials photos: Mighty Media, Inc.

Design Elements Shutterstock: KALYA MALYA, lukeruk, sherilhome

All the internet addresses (URLs) given in this book were valid at the time of going to press. However, due to the dynamic nature of the internet, some addresses may have changed, or sites may have changed or ceased to exist since publication. While the author and publisher regret any inconvenience this may cause readers, no responsibility for any such changes can be accepted by either the author or the publisher.

Printed and bound in India

CONTENTS

Autumn..4

Black History Month.....................6

Sukkot...8

Rosh Hashanah..........................10

Navaratri.....................................12

World Mental Health Day..........14

Indigenous Peoples' Day...........16

Seasonal craft............................18

Day of the Dead.........................20

Thanksgiving..............................22

Diwali...24

Seasonal craft............................26

Halloween...................................28

   Find out more........................32

   About the author...................32

Autumn

What is your favourite part of autumn? Is it the new stationery for school or the colourful leaves? Maybe it's all the seasonal celebrations, including Halloween, Rosh Hashanah and Thanksgiving!

Celebrate autumn with cool projects that reflect the season. Create a floating light for Diwali or a citrus-stamped towel for Sukkot. You can even build a glowing sugar skull for Day of the Dead or a nature mosaic for Indigenous Peoples' Day. Autumn is filled with enough natural beauty and festivities to keep you crafting all season long!

BASIC SUPPLIES

beads

cardboard

craft glue

crayons

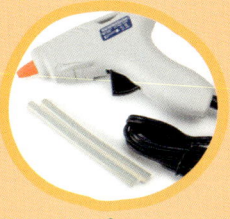
hot glue gun

paint and paintbrushes

ruler

scissors

string

wool

CRAFTING TIPS

Be prepared! Read through the list of materials and instructions before starting a project. Cover your workspace with paper or plastic to protect it from messes or spills.

Think outside the book! Lots of the projects in this book use materials you'll probably find around your home. Is there something you can't find? Think of ways to adapt the project using items you do have.

Ask first! Get permission before using materials you find at home or school. Also, ask before you collect items from nature and bring them indoors.

Be safe! Ask an adult for help with projects that require sharp or hot tools.

Clean up! When your project is complete, put all materials and tools back where you found them. Clean up any spills and wipe down your crafting surface.

BLACK HISTORY MONTH
Black History bunting

October is Black History Month in the UK. It's a time to reflect on the history and celebrate the achievements and contributions of black people in society. Decorate your space with red, green, black and gold bunting as a tribute to Black history!

What you need

- ruler
- marker pen
- cardboard
- scissors
- red, green, black and gold fabric (or card)
- string
- hot glue gun
- internet access

What you do

1. Use a ruler and marker pen to draw a triangle on cardboard. It should have a 13-cm (5-in) base and 19-cm (7.5-in) sides. Cut out the triangle.

2. Trace the cardboard template on scraps of red, green, black and gold fabric (or card) to make as many flags as you like. Cut out the flags.

3. Cut a piece of string the desired length of your bunting. For eight flags, you'll want about (165 cm) (65 in) of string.

4. Space the flags evenly along the string. Attach the flags to the string with hot glue.

5. Search online for quotes by well-known Black people. Choose your favourite quotes and write them on a few or all of the flags.

6. Hang your Black History bunting for all to see!

SUKKOT
Citrus stamp tea towel

A citrus fruit called the etrog is an important symbol during Sukkot, a Jewish festival of gratitude. But you can use any citrus fruit to make a homemade citrus stamp. Use it to refresh and brighten up a plain old tea towel!

What you need

- lemon, lime, orange or other citrus fruit
- sharp cutting knife
- small bowl
- paring knife
- kitchen roll
- fabric paint and paintbrush
- pie tin or small tray
- cotton tea towel

What you do

1. Ask an adult to help you cut the citrus fruit in half. Save one of the halves for cooking or baking.

2. Gently squeeze the other half over a bowl to remove some of the juice. It's okay if you don't get all the juice out. Refrigerate the juice for cooking or baking.

3. Ask an adult to help you carefully carve out the segments of flesh in your squeezed fruit half. Make sure you keep the walls between each section intact. Eat the cut-out sections or save them for later!

4. Use kitchen roll to clean up any excess juice or pulp on the fruit half. Then let the fruit half dry out, cut-end up, for about 15 minutes.

5. Spread a thin layer of fabric paint over the bottom of a pie tin or small tray. Dip the flat end of the fruit half in the paint. Make a few practice stamps on kitchen roll.

6. Lay the tea towel flat on a protected surface. Use your citrus stamp to decorate the towel in any pattern you like.

7. Let the towel dry. Then display it where everyone can see!

ROSH HASHANAH
Wool apples

Rosh Hashanah is the Jewish New Year. It takes place in September or October. During this holiday, many people eat apples dipped in honey to symbolize hope for a sweet new year. Decorate your table with cute wool apples in honour of Rosh Hashanah!

What you need

- cardboard
- ruler
- scissors
- balls of red and/or green wool
- string
- green leaves (real or artificial)

What you do

1. Cut a rectangle of cardboard that is 7.5 centimetres (3 inches) wide and 10 cm (4 in) long.

2. Wrap the wool around the width of the cardboard about 100 times, unravelling it from the ball as you go.

3. When you have finished wrapping, cut the wool off the ball. Carefully pull the wrapped wool off the cardboard so it keeps its shape.

4. Cut a 25.5-cm (10-inch) piece of wool. Slip the piece through the centre of the wrapped wool and knot to secure. This will create an apple shape. Don't cut off the extra tied wool.

5. Cut a 25.5-cm (10-in) piece of string. Lay the string across the knot you made in step 4. Secure the string to the apple using the extra length of wool.

6. Tie about eight knots into the string to create the apple's stem.

7. Use the extra wool to tie the leaf to the base of the stem. Then cut off any remaining bits of wool and string.

8. Repeat steps 2 to 7 to make more apples for your table!

NAVARATRI
Dandiya sticks

Navaratri is a Hindu festival celebrating the triumph of good over evil. Many people celebrate Navaratri with a traditional dance called Dandiya. Dancers hold sticks that represent swords. Make your own Dandiya sticks out of newspaper and ribbons!

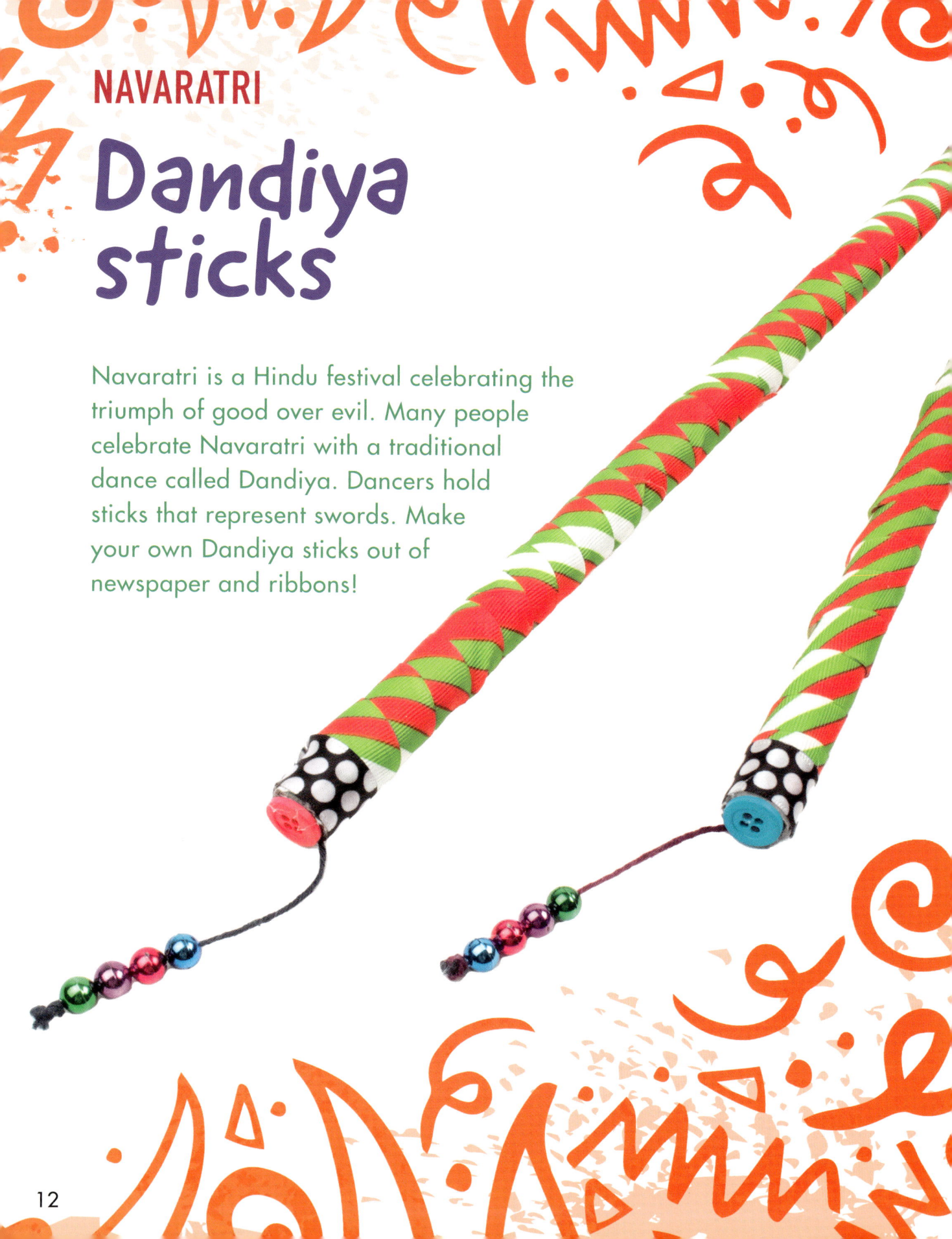

What you need

- newspaper
- wooden skewer
- glue stick
- scissors
- ruler
- hot glue gun
- ribbon
- string
- beads
- buttons

What you do

1. Lay a sheet of newspaper flat. Starting at one corner, begin to tightly roll the newspaper around a wooden skewer. Slide the skewer out once you've started the roll. Continue rolling. Spread glue onto the newspaper every few rolls until you reach the other corner. Glue the corner in place.

2. Lay another sheet of newspaper flat. Glue the middle of the roll you made to a corner of the new sheet. Roll the sheets together to build on the original roll. Glue the opposite corner in place.

3. Cut the ends of the newspaper roll so it is 35 centimetres (14 in) long. This is your dandiya stick!

4. Hot-glue the end of a ribbon to one end of your dandiya stick. Wrap the ribbon around the stick, gluing every several centimetres, until all the newspaper is covered.

5. Cut a 15-cm (6-in) piece of string and tie a knot at one end. Thread beads onto the string.

6. Hot-glue the unknotted end of the string to one end of your Dandiya stick. Use buttons and glue to cap both ends of the stick.

7. Repeat steps 1 to 6 to make a second Dandiya stick. Now you are ready to dance!

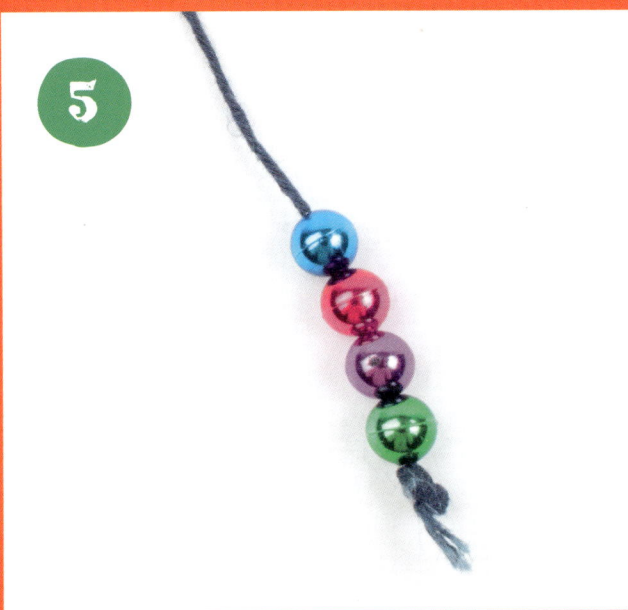

WORLD MENTAL HEALTH DAY

Soothing foam slime

World Mental Health Day takes place in October. Why not look after your own mental health with a few mindful minutes? This foam slime will help focus your senses and calm your mind.

What you need

- measuring cup and spoons
- bicarbonate of soda
- water
- bowls
- craft stick for mixing
- craft glue
- food colouring
- foam beads

What you do

1. Pour half a teaspoon of bicarbonate of soda into 240 ml warm water. Stir until the bicarbonate of soda dissolves. Set the solution aside.

2. In a bowl, mix 240 ml craft glue and 240 ml water. Mix food colouring into the glue mixture until you've reached your desired colour.

3. Add 45 g of the bicarbonate of soda solution to the glue mixture. Mix in more solution a spoonful at a time until you've created a mass of slime.

4. Pour 470 g of foam beads into a second large bowl. Add the slime to the second bowl and begin mixing in the beads.

5. Keep adding more foam beads, a little bit at a time, until the slime cannot hold any more.

6. Play with your slime! Notice how it feels and sounds as you squeeze it. Wash your hands after handling the slime.

INDIGENOUS PEOPLES' DAY

Natural state mosaic

Indigenous Peoples' Day honours Native Americans and their histories. As the first inhabitants of what is now the United States, Native people lived off the land around them. Gather bits of nature to make a mosaic of your country. Then research the nations and tribes that first settled in the land you live on.

What you need

- cardboard
- scissors
- ruler
- paint (brown, white) and paintbrushes
- pencil
- collected bits of nature, such as twigs and dandelions
- hot glue gun
- string
- push pin
- split pin

What you do

1. Cut a piece of cardboard 32 cm (12.5 in) long and 26.5 cm (10.5 in) wide.

2. Paint the cardboard. To make it look like whitewashed wood, paint a layer of brown and then white. Let the paint dry after each layer.

3. Sketch or trace an outline of your country on the cardboard.

4. Arrange collected pieces of nature within the outline of your county or region. Glue them on.

5. Cut a 30-cm (12-in) piece of string. Knot the ends together to make a loop.

6. Use the push pin to make a hole near the top of your artwork.

7. Push the split pin through the hole. Slip the string loop around the fastener legs. Flatten the legs against the cardboard. Your mosaic is ready to hang up!

SEASONAL CRAFT
Autumn fairy

Autumn is a time of dramatic transformation in nature. Trees burst into fiery colours. Leaves fall and branches turn bare. Go on an autumn walk to collect bits of nature. Then use these pieces to create a fairy in honour of the season!

What you need

- collected bits of nature, such as acorns, twigs and stones
- hot glue gun
- tweezers (optional)

What you do

1. Select an item that could be the body of your fairy, such as a pine cone or piece of birch bark.

2. Select an item to be your fairy's head, such as an acorn or stone.

3. Glue the fairy's head to its body.

4. Glue twigs or winged seeds to the body for arms or wings.

5. Add any final embellishments, such as a flower petal hat, to your fairy. Use tweezers to help transfer flower buds and other small materials as needed.

6. Glue your finished fairy to a stone or bark base so it can stand on its own!

19

DAY OF THE DEAD
Glowing skulls

Day of the Dead is a Mexican holiday celebrated in early November. According to tradition, the spirits of loved ones rejoin their families on this day. Many people celebrate by painting skulls on their faces or decorating their homes with sugar skulls. Make your own glowing skulls using plastic eggs and LEDs!

Fun fact

In Spanish, Day of the Dead is known as Día de los Muertos.

What you need

- black paint and paintbrush
- LED tea lights
- plastic eggs
- push pin
- screwdriver
- pliers
- black permanent marker pen
- images of sugar skulls (optional)
- hot glue gun (optional)

What you do

1. Paint the bases of the LED lights black. Let them dry.

2. Ask an adult to help you poke several holes in the top of a plastic egg using a push pin. Have the adult use a screwdriver to expand the small holes into one big hole.

3. Have the adult use pliers to expand the hole even more. It should be large enough to fit the flame of an LED tea light.

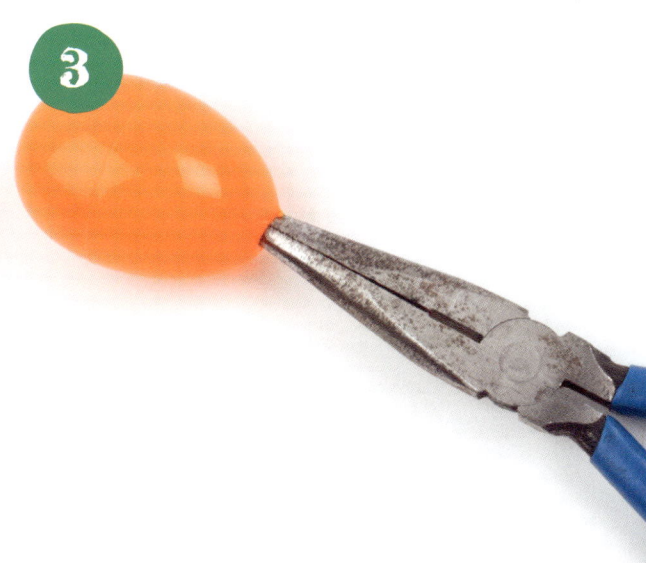

4. Use a black permanent marker to draw a skull on the plastic egg. Add details like leaves, dots, hearts and flowers. If you like, look up images of sugar skulls on the internet for inspiration.

5. Push an LED tea light's flame into the hole. If you like, hot-glue the egg to the light base. Turn on the LED to make your skull glow.

6. Repeat steps 2 to 5 to make more glowing skulls!

THANKSGIVING
Crayon-drip pumpkin

Thanksgiving is a US harvest celebration that dates back to colonial America. Historians say pumpkin was on the table at the first Thanksgiving meal in Plymouth, Massachusetts. Pumpkins remain a popular symbol of the autumn harvest. Today, many Thanksgiving feasts include pumpkin pie!

Fun fact
Potatoes of all kinds are another popular Thanksgiving dish. But historians say this root vegetable would not have been on the menu at the first Thanksgiving.

What you need

- crayons
- craft knife
- hot glue gun
- white pumpkin
- newspaper
- hair dryer

What you do

1. Pick out crayon colours to paint your pumpkin with. Peel the paper off the crayons. Break each crayon into pieces about 1.3 cm (½ in) to 4 cm (1.5 in) long. Use long pieces for a large pumpkin and short pieces for a small pumpkin.

2. Ask an adult to help you cut the crayon pieces in half lengthwise with a craft knife. This helps the crayons melt faster.

3. Hot-glue the crayon pieces around the pumpkin stem, flat sides down.

4. Place the pumpkin on a large surface covered in newspaper.

5. Hold a hair dryer about 8 cm (3 in) above the crayons to melt them. On the hair dryer's highest setting, this will take about 5 minutes. It will take longer if the crayon pieces are long or thick.

6. Let the crayon wax dry. Then put your pumpkin on display!

DIWALI
Floating light

Diwali is often called the Festival of Lights. It's a time for gathering and exchanging gifts with loved ones. During the five-day celebration, clay lamps fill homes and temples with light. You can use a glass jar and beads to create a colourful floating light in honour of Diwali!

Fun fact

Diwali is a major holiday in India, where most of the population is Hindu. But it's celebrated across the world by people who practise Hinduism, Jainism or Sikhism.

What you need

- glass jar with lid
- hammer and nail
- paint and paintbrush (optional)
- craft wire
- ruler
- wire cutter
- pliers
- hot glue gun and/or craft glue and paintbrush
- beads
- tweezers (optional)
- LED tea light

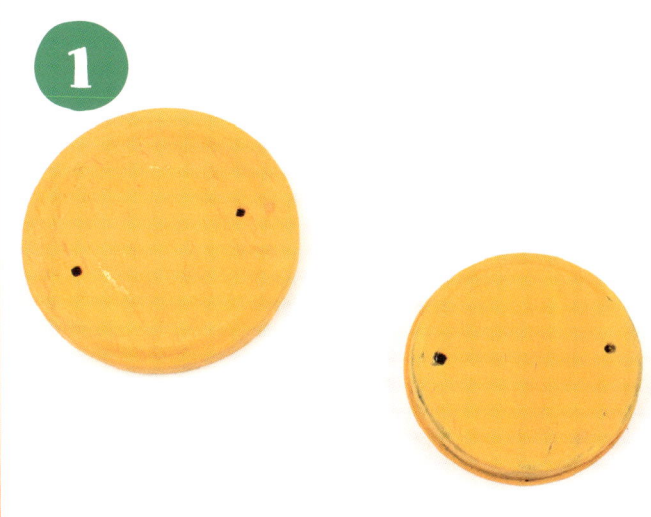

What you do

1. Ask an adult to poke two holes in the lid of a jar, one near each edge, using a hammer and nail. If you like, paint the lid a colour of your choice. Let the paint dry.

2. Cut a 20-cm (8-in) piece of craft wire. Put each end of the wire into a hole in the lid to form a handle. Use pliers to tightly loop the wire ends on the underside of the lid.

3. Cover the surface of the jar with beads. If you are using tiny beads, paint regular craft glue onto the jar and roll the jar over the beads. If you are using large beads, attach them to the jar with hot glue and tweezers.

4. Place an LED tea light in the jar and close the lid. Then hang up your floating light!

SEASONAL CRAFT
Pine cone wreath

Putting up a wreath is a simple way to celebrate any season. Give your door a golden autumnal glow with this wreath made of painted pine cones!

Fun fact

A pine cone's purpose is to house seeds. Its scales stay closed to keep the seeds safe from cold or damp weather. When the weather turns warm and dry, the scales open to spread the seeds!

What you need

- about 50 pine cones of various sizes
- paint (red, orange, yellow) and paintbrushes
- craft glue
- floral foam ring, either 25 or 30.5 cm (10 or 12 in)
- newspaper
- ruler
- scissors
- string
- hot glue gun

What you do

1. Paint the tips of the pine cone scales red, orange and yellow. Let them dry.

2. Spread craft glue over the floral foam ring. Wrap the foam in newspaper. This creates a bulkier surface to glue the pine cones to.

3. Cut a 60-cm (24-in) piece of string. Knot the ends of the string together to form a big loop. Wrap the string loop around the ring to make a hanger.

4. Glue the pine cones to the ring. Start with the largest pine cones. Then fill in the gaps with smaller pine cones until your wreath looks full.

5. Hang up your wreath using the string loop!

HALLOWEEN
Sticky spider's web

Halloween dates back to an ancient Celtic festival where people wore costumes to hide from ghosts. Dressing up in costume is still a very popular Halloween tradition. So is putting up spooky decorations, like this creepy spider's web!

What you need

- medium bowl
- craft glue
- water
- measuring cup and spoon
- paint (optional)
- mixing spoon
- wool
- ruler
- scissors
- tape
- wax paper
- pipe cleaners
- beads
- hot glue gun
- fishing line

What you do

1. Mix 60 ml (2 fl oz) craft glue and 15 ml (0.5 fl oz) water in a medium bowl. If you want a coloured web, mix in a few drops of paint too.

2. Cut four 40-cm (16-in) lengths of wool and six 75-cm (30-in) lengths of wool.

3. Tape together two sheets of wax paper and lay them on your work surface. Make sure the wax paper surface is big enough to fit one 40-cm (16-in) length of wool vertically and horizontally.

4. Dip the four 40-cm (16-in) lengths of wool into the glue mixture so they are completely covered.

5. Pull each wool piece out, lightly pulling them between two fingers to remove excess glue.

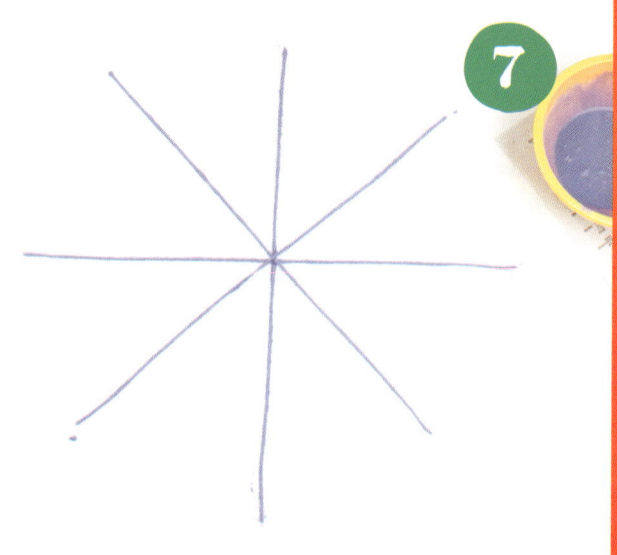

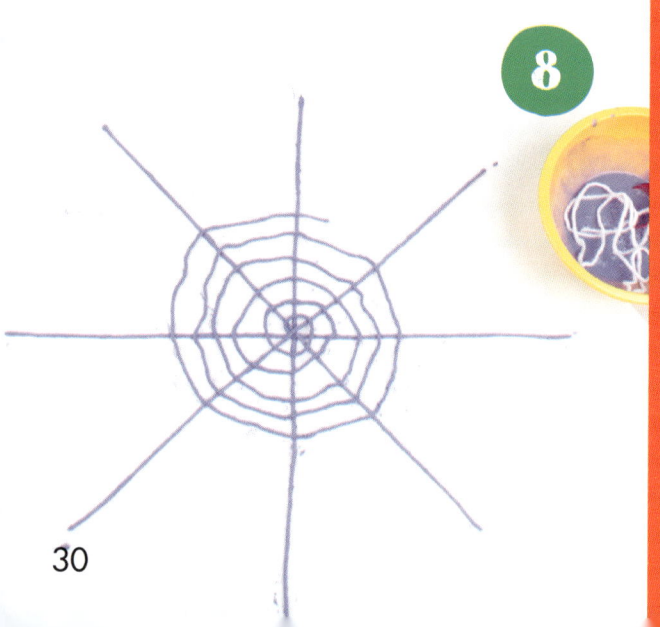

6. Place two glue-covered lengths of wool in the shape of a plus sign onto the wax paper.

7. Place the other two glue-covered lengths of wool in the shape of an X over the first shape.

8. Repeat steps 4 and 5 with a 75-cm (30-in) length of wool. Starting at the centre of your web shape, lay the wool over the web so it spirals out towards the open ends. When you reach the end of a length of wool, cover the next piece with glue and start where the previous piece left off. Once the web is complete, let it dry for up to 24 hours.

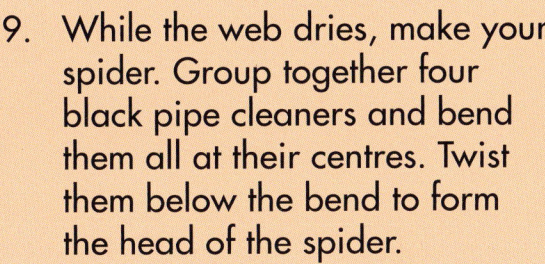

9. While the web dries, make your spider. Group together four black pipe cleaners and bend them all at their centres. Twist them below the bend to form the head of the spider.

10. Separate the eight stem ends into two groups of four. These are your spider's legs.

11. Thread two yellow beads onto each leg. Bend the leg at each bead.

12. Once the web is dry, carefully remove it from the wax paper. Use hot glue to reconnect any portions that have come apart.

13. Use fishing line to hang up the web. Then place your spider in the centre!

FIND OUT MORE

BOOKS

10-Minute Crafty Projects (10-Minute Makers), Elsie Olson (Raintree, 2022)

Celebrations Around the World (Customs Around the World), Wil Mara (Raintree, 2021)

Diwali (Traditions and Celebrations), Anita Nahta Amin (Raintree, 2022)

WEBSITES

learnenglishkids.britishcouncil.org/category/topics/festivals-and-celebrations
Find out about different world festivals and celebrations as well as some craft activities on this website.

www.bbc.co.uk/cbbc/curations/bp-arts-and-crafts-collection
CBBC has lots of craft ideas you can make.

ABOUT THE AUTHOR

Megan Borgert-Spaniol is an author and editor of children's media. When she isn't writing or reading, she enjoys doing yoga, eating croissants and making homemade pizzas. Megan lives in Minneapolis, Minnesota, USA, with a tall, goofy man and a small, chatty cat.